My Grandma Has Alzheimer's

By Lola Carlile

Illustrations by Joann Sands

An interactive picture book.
Research has shown that comprehending concepts better occurs when multi-modalities are utilized. Those research-based ideas are employed at the end of this book.

My Grandma Has Alzheimer's
Copyright 2014 by Lola Carlile. All rights reserved.

No part of this publication may be reproduced, stored in a retrieval system or transmitted in any way by any means, electronic, photocopy, recording or otherwise without the prior permission of the author except as provided by USA copyright law.

Published by Masabi Press
PO Box 2663
Salem, Oregon 97308
United States

Masabi Press is dedicated to promoting excellence in literacy.

ISBN-13: 978-1507643501

ISBN-10: 1507643500

1. Juvenile Fiction/Social Issues/Alzheimer's/
2. Juvenile Fiction/Elderly/Grandparents

Dedicated to Grandma Betty, her seven children, and many grandchildren and great-grandchildren.

Thanks to my youngest son for inspiring me to write this book to help others who are feeling the mystery of Alzheimer's. May this book help to reaffirm that no matter what happens, Alzheimer's does not take our love away!

To all those families afflicted with this illness, may your days be blessed with smiles, hugs, great art and music.

My Grandma Has Alzheimer's

Betty Rae is 90 years old today. She is my short and very spunky grandmother. All her grandchildren and great grandchildren like to hug her. She sparkles when she speaks. Her voice is bright and tinny.

She loves everyone. She has Alzheimer's. No one wants to talk about it much. My aunts and uncles and parents are in denial. "She is just forgetful." "She is depressed." But we sense something is wrong. And it is a disease called Alzheimer's.

Alzheimer's is a disease people can get at any age. For most people, Alzheimer's attacks after they are fifty years old. But thirty year olds can get it, too. It is a disease that takes people's memories away.

It begins slowly and people can live for several decades with it. Grandma Betty has been diagnosed with Alzheimer's for more than two decades – that is twenty years!

Grandma Betty always forgot things. That's not why she has Alzheimer's. We all forget things. But Grandma Betty now forgets things we all know. Like Grandpa Al died three years ago.

Grandma thinks she just ate dinner with him. But she didn't. She just can't remember.

I don't quite know how to talk with Grandma anymore. What should I say when she says Grandpa is somewhere? What should I answer when she asks me what grade I am in for the hundredth time? I usually just smile and not try to correct her. Why get her upset? The caretakers and others tell me I am right to do so.

She says naughty things sometimes that kind of make us laugh. Until I remember...that my Grandma would never have really said naughty things. It is her disease that is making her say those things. It is not Grandma's fault.

I like to visit her and tell her she is doing the best she can. She apologizes sometimes to me. She says she is sorry she can't remember things. I just hug her and say that is okay. I say she is a good and loving woman. I am so glad she is my grandmother.

She always liked to learn and now is no different.

Mom brought her a picture book about squid. We watched a short video about the giant squid. It can grow up to sixty feet long. We ooohed and aaahed at the

picture. Grandma liked it a lot. Even though sometimes she got up and did something else. She liked the book better. We left the squid book with her.

Grandma gets her nails done. She likes really bright and flashy colors now. She didn't used to. But I think they look great. Go, Grandma, go!

She likes to shove things into her purse at the home. We looked for days for some of these things until one of my aunts found the lost items in her purse. In her purse. In the closet. The purse she does not use any longer.

Dad cleans her kitchen when we go to visit. It's filled with gross stuff. Grandma proudly says she doesn't clean anymore. Boy, that's the truth! Dad can't stand the stench. We laugh as we talk with Grandma. She is here now. We love to look at her.

When we take Grandma to a restaurant she gets nervous. All the noise startles her. She does not know what to order.

So we order for her. Dad says she just likes meat and potatoes. We order her fried chicken strips and potatoes and gravy. She eats half and wants to save the rest. Mom puts the leftovers in a box and writes the date on top. That is so Grandma won't forget how old the food is and eat bad food later on...

The other day Grandma complained to my aunt that she had met a very nice lady, but that lady would not come into her apartment.

Aunt Sandy asked Grandma to show her the lady. As they were getting ready to go out the door to the hallway, Grandma smiled and pointed. Aunt Sandy looked and saw Grandma's reflection in the mirror. "See? She is waving at me, but she just won't come in."

Aunt Sandy sighed. Yes, Grandma thought her reflection was another person.

Grandma loves to eat pie. Dad says she was the best pie baker of all times.

He gets a little tear in his eye as he tells her that she used to bake the best pies in the world. She smiles. I think she understands.

She lives in an apartment they call assisted living. At first I thought it looked like a really nice dorm room. My sister and brother lived in a college dorm that was not that nice. Mom joked she was even a little jealous – Grandma did not have to cook or clean – all she had to do was wake up and go on field trips. That was before we found out that she has Alzheimer's.

I wonder if Grandma is lonely. I know I am afraid. I don't know what is coming next. Someone said that this is a long good-bye to Grandma. She is slowly slipping away, they say. No one knows how long she will still recognize us. They say one day she won't. Some people even get depressed and mad. They yell because they don't understand what is going on with their minds.

Grandma is not there yet. She still knows most of her grandchildren. She forgets what we do, but she recognizes our faces. She will always be my grandma, no matter what. She can change all she wants, but I have pictures and memories of her. I know who she is. And when she no longer knows who I am, I will still go see her and hug her and tell her stories. Her little soft hugs and chirpy little voice will forever be in my memories.

Prayer For Grandma

Dear God,

I know that you are really busy, but I want to just tell you about someone. You may know her as Betty Rae, but she is just Grandma Betty to me. She is a good woman. She always worked hard. She was a good mom and grandma. She was a good wife, too. Please bless her and make her illness easier for her to bear. And when you take her to heaven, please make sure you find Grandpa Al for her, so they can be together forever.

Thank you,
Just a Grandchild

What did you think of the story?

Describe or draw Grandma Betty.

Draw a picture of the child who is telling the story.

How would you feel or how do you feel about someone you love having Alzheimer's? Write words or just draw your feelings below.

Things you can do with your Grandparents or other loved ones:
- Read short stories to them
- Talk about what you read
- Draw or just scribble
- Do crossword puzzles
- Do word searches
- Sing songs
- Make a recipe together
- Color in a coloring book
- Look at leaves
- Draw leaves
- Make something with play doh
- Roll a ball across the table (be sure you don't throw it!)
- Look at animal pictures
- Talk about the holiday

About the Author

Lola Carlile is an educator, writer, and art therapist. She has been a writer for most of her life. She is the author of five books. This is her first picture book.

Her life's goal is to make life just a bit better in the moment for each person she meets. Carlile lives in the United States with her husband and is the mother of three grown men and proud grandma of a darling granddaughter and a sweet grandson.

About the Illustrator

Joann Sands has been painting since she was a young girl. She is self-taught and has, over the years, painted in many mediums and styles. It's a real passion for her which takes her into a world of color and imagination.

She has held solo exhibits in Spain and throughout the UK. She likes to bring laughter and happiness to her paintings and illustrations for adults and children to enjoy. She lives in England with her husband Rex.

Printed in Great Britain
by Amazon.co.uk, Ltd.,
Marston Gate.